Australian
WEDDING
TOASTS AND SPEECHES

With thanks:

The publishers would like to thank Mr. Mark Bowmer for his editorial contribution
and proof reading of this publication.

First published in 1996 by Worsthorne Pedersen Publishing Pty Ltd
Kangaloon Road, East Kangaloon NSW 2576 Ph: 048 88 2377 Fax: 048 88 2245

Distribution enquiries:

Victoria: Worsthorne Publishing: (03) 9787 2144
All other areas: Worsthorne Pedersen Publishing Pty Ltd: (048) 88 2377

ISBN 0 646 27448 1

CONTENTS

TOASTS & SPEECHES	4
TRADITIONAL ORDER OF SPEECHES	7
MASTER OF CEREMONIES	10
PREPARING YOUR SPEECH	13
DELIVERING YOUR SPEECH	18
ON THE DAY	27
OPENING LINES FOR YOUR SPEECH	30
POPULAR QUOTATIONS	35
WEDDING JOKES	38
THE SPEECHES	40
FATHER OF THE BRIDE	41
BRIDE AND GROOM	51
BEST MAN	66
THE WEDDING	76
ORDER OF TOASTS AND SPEECHES	79
IMPORTANT INFORMATION	81
MY SPEECH	82
NOTES	86

TOASTS & SPEECHES

♦

The toasts and speeches are a highlight of any wedding and should be given much attention in the pre-wedding planning stages.

Most guests eagerly look forward to this event, expecting to hear a mix of speeches that bring a touch of humour and sincerity to the occasion.

A well organised bride and groom will carefully discuss the expectations they have about the speeches for their wedding.

It is no good ignoring the speeches and then being disappointed on the night.

Many people cringe when they hear the question: "Would you mind giving a speech at our wedding?" This is due to the fact that they have anxieties (usually unfounded) about how they will perform as a public speaker.

To help alleviate this we we have written this book so a copy may be given to each speaker at your wedding.

Your own set of circumstances will dictate how you want the speeches presented at your wedding.

~ This book is designed to take some of the difficulty out of speech preparation and delivery. ~

♦

You will need to consider such questions as: how many speakers are to appear at your wedding, your personal and traditional religious requirements, family circumstances and the degree of formality of the wedding.

With these in mind, this book has been designed so that you can easily adapt it to your individual circumstances.

It is a good idea to meet with all speakers before the wedding day, including the bride's father, and discuss with them any requirements you may have.

Make a list of everything and anything that is important to you both, and give this to each speaker for their reference.

Detail all people who should be included for special thanks and indicate the theme of your wedding.

Any special family circumstances should be noted (divorced parents, a deceased member of the family, etc.) as well as any embarrassing information that definitely should not be mentioned.

If the Best Man is to perform the duty of Master of Ceremonies, it is wise to ensure that he is confident of the task.

If he is a rather shy person, it might be a good idea to use someone who is naturally more confident, otherwise the toasts and speeches may not flow smoothly.

You may even decide to

~ *Detail carefully all people who should be included for special thanks.* ~

5

◆

hire a professional M.C. for this role.

It is important to make the speakers at your wedding feel comfortable.

They should have somewhere central to stand so they do not have to shout to be heard.

If you have a microphone, ensure it is not poking in the speakers' faces and can be adjusted accordingly.

Supply a glass of water in case they suddenly find themselves with a dry throat and ensure it is within easy reach.

Introduce the speakers to each other at the beginning of the reception if they do not know each other.

That way they will feel comfortable with the order of things.

No speech should embarrass, ridicule, condemn or be overtly suggestive.

Bad language and vulgarity is definitely out and will not be well received.

Your speech should ensure that all guests are left feeling warm towards you and your speakers.

In this way they will enjoy the romance of the occasion and feel involved in a true celebration of your marriage!

NOTES

TRADITIONAL ORDER OF SPEECHES

◆

The toasts and speeches are a traditional part of the reception festivities and much looked forward to by most guests.

They are usually made before the coffee stage of the meal and after the cutting of the cake.

The Best Man or Master of Ceremonies controls the overall flow of events and begins by politely calling the guests to attention.

He/she then calls upon the bride's father to propose a toast to the health and happiness of the bride and groom.

FATHER OF THE BRIDE

This speech usually commences with the father of the bride talking about his daughter. It may include amusing things that happened in her childhood, as well as antics from her teenage years and her growth into adulthood.

He may go on to relate how he has come to know the groom, welcome him into the family and say how delighted he and his wife are at the joining of the couple in marriage.

At this point, he may ask his wife to say a few

> ~ *The speeches are usually held before the coffee stage of the meal and after the cutting of the cake.* ~

words.

This is an increasingly popular extension to the father of the bride speech and usually much enjoyed by guests.

He then concludes his speech by offering a toast to the bride and groom.

BRIDEGROOM

The bridegroom replies to the father of the bride speech, thanks the bride's parents for the wedding and says how entirely memorable the whole occasion has been.

He thanks his own parents for his upbringing and talks a little about himself and his bride, perhaps quoting some humorous incident from their courtship to add to the flavour of the speech.

It is also important to thank the best man, ushers and anyone who has assisted with the planning of the wedding.

It has also become popular for the bridegroom to call on the bride to give her own speech.

She joins her husband on the podium where she also gives thanks to her parents for the wedding, talks of her fondness for her family-in-law, and of the groom and their new life together.

Finally, she too thanks everyone who has been involved with the wedding, especially the bridesmaids, before referring the continuation of the speeches back to the groom.

The bridegroom then proposes a toast to the bridesmaids, thanking them for all the help and support extended to his bride. It is also usual to comment on how beautiful they look and wish them good health with the raising of glasses.

BEST MAN

The best man speaks after the bridegroom. It is his duty to reply on behalf of the bridesmaids. He goes on to thank the groom for asking him to be best man. He may speak of his friendship with the groom and include some anecdotes of their adventures when single.

At this point, the best man reads out any messages received and concludes by inviting all guests to enjoy the rest of the evening. (The traditional "telegram" is no longer possible although a *lettergram* service is available through Australia Post. Often today facsimile messages are sent directly to the reception venue.)

The official reception formalities are now concluded.

The rest of the event adopts a more relaxed approach with the bride and groom attempting to have a few words with as many guests as possible. Dancing is enjoyed by all guests who can now "let their hair down".

A MODERN APPROACH

There is a growing trend for couples to decide who they wish to deliver a speech at their wedding, breaking from the traditional formula.

It may be decided to include the mother of the bride or groom, matron of honour, the officiator of the ceremony or any other person of choice.

When breaking from tradition it is important not to lose sight of the toasts. They are still a necessity and punctuate all events with the raising of glasses. This involves the guests firsthand in the celebration.

MASTER OF CEREMONIES

♦

The Master of Ceremonies' primary duty is to act as the intermediary between the toasts and speeches during the wedding reception.

This role may be extended to introduce each guest as they arrive, although this generally only applies if a receiving line has been organised by the bride and groom, or at state weddings.

The M.C. is usually a relative or close friend of the family in which case you will know the wedding party personally. This obviously can make the job a whole lot easier. If not, it is important to familiarise yourself with the wedding party and the speakers at the reception.

If at all possible, try to organise a pre-wedding social get-together to meet all of the speakers. This will make your role a lot easier on the day.

If it is not possible to meet everyone beforehand then simply introduce yourself at the beginning of the reception, making it clear that you are the M.C.

> *~ The M.C. is usually a relative or close friend of the family, in which case he/she will know the wedding party personally. ~*

◆

Prior to the wedding, the bride or bride's mother will usually provide you with the names of all the people who will be speaking, their relationship to the bride and groom and the toast or speech for which they will be responsible.

At the reception you should make yourself known to the function organiser to co-ordinate: the timing of speeches, champagne for the toasts and to check that everything is at the ready, such as a knife for the cutting of the cake.

You should also make yourself known to the musicians and ensure the appropriate music is available for the bridal waltz.

Once dessert has been served you should introduce yourself to the gathering, calling the guests to attention.

Remember, you are largely responsible for the flow of events once the toasts begin.

You may also be called upon to propose a toast to the Bride and Groom.

A word of warning, don't take over and dominate the reception. The reception venue will already have an expert that is well used to co-ordinating wedding procedure. You should take directions from this person as they can best advise you.

In planning what to say as the M.C., both as an introduction to the speeches and between each speech, use the

~ *The M.C. is largely responsible for the overall flow of events during the reception.* ~

◆

guidelines in this book. You may decide to have a serious approach or a humorous one.

It is important to be consistent as it is your role to ensure the proceedings retain a feeling of continuity.

Anecdotes and jokes are especially appropriate for the M.C. to use. They may act as fillers between the actual speeches or may offer light relief if any speech is excessively heavy and over-emotional. The only word of caution, shy away from vulgarity or anything that may offend or embarrass. You do not wish to turn the audience against you, which can happen if you have said something in obvious bad taste.

Do not speak for too long. Approximately two minutes when you first speak and one minute between speeches should be the maximum.

What you plan to say should be concise and well worded and it is important to wear a happy, smiling expression.

You should be well groomed and well dressed. Finally, the most important thing to remember is to be at the right place at the right time!

NOTES

Preparing Your Speech

◆

So, you have been asked to give a speech at a wedding. You may feel nervous or excited by the prospect and think to yourself: "What do I do now?" There is only one answer....BE PREPARED!

Preparation, Planning & Practise

Preparation is absolutely vital to the success of your speech. Good preparation, planning and practise will give you the confidence to deliver the speech in a relaxed manner. This will calm your nerves and heighten your enjoyment of the experience.

Sample Speeches

Before you even begin to consider the wedding speech you are to prepare, carefully read the sample speeches provided in this book.

They are sure to give you ideas which will become invaluable as you begin to personalise your own speech.

This is the perfect place to begin, alleviating a lot of wasted time.

Be Yourself

Consider your role within the wedding party. Are

> ~ *Preparation, planning and practise is absolutely vital to the success of your speech.* ~

♦

you the father of the bride, the groom, the bride, the best man, or a family friend.

Why have you been asked to give a speech?

What can you bring to the wedding celebrations? Are you witty, serious minded or aloof? How will this affect your speech.

Do not attempt a highly amusing speech if you tend to be a serious person. You will find this uncomfortable and more likely than not, fail to produce the desired effect.

By the same token if you are known by all as a real joker, do not attempt a flowery, gushing speech. It may appear insincere.

Write your speech to suite your personality and style and it will be a success.

OUTLINE THE DETAIL

Planning your speech should begin with a notepaper and pen.

Firstly, write down the names of the couple getting married. This will help you personalise your ideas through a mental image of the individuals involved.

To extend this idea, jot down as much information about the wedding and the people involved as you can. This might include family background, religion, nationality, venue, formality of the wedding, etc.

Give yourself a total mental image of the people and wedding involved and all that this brings to mind.

> ~ *Write your speech to suit your personality and style and it will be a success..* ~

CONTENT

An interesting speech delivers new information. If at all possible, take a little time to get to know the families of the bride and groom, their heritage or even what the family name means.

Research can mean freedom, giving you lots of interesting content for your speech.

HOW LONG SHOULD YOU SPEAK?

Do not become long-winded and drawn out, as people will lose interest. Approximately three to five minutes is a good length of time. You can extend your speech only for very formal weddings.

INTERESTING DETAIL TO INCLUDE

Look for interesting material from the lives of the bride and groom relating to their professions, travel, hobbies, interests and aspirations. Think of how they met and how long they have been courting. Include anecdotes of their relationship, interesting personality traits, things you admire and stories you would like to tell. Be kind, generous and tactful!

IMAGINE WHAT THEY WOULD LIKE YOU TO SAY AND WHO THEY WOULD LIKE YOU TO TALK ABOUT!

Further to this, gather snippets of information that can be included in your speech.

Jokes and quotations are often useful and can be

> *~ Approximately three to five minutes is a good length of time for a wedding speech. ~*

◆

used as fillers between ideas within the speech. Scan through and delete anything that sounds either indiscreet or downright rude. Avoid blatant sexual innuendoes and crude jokes. Look for items that may cause embarrassment and remove them.

Ensure that you have not used any slang or swear words as they are totally unacceptable for the occasion of a wedding.

A ROUGH DRAFT BEGINS TO FORM

To flow smoothly the content of the speech must be arranged in a logical order.

Write down essentials that must be included. These may be people you must specifically thank, or a toast you must include.

Arrange your notes in the order that you would like the content to be delivered. The skeleton of the speech will begin to take shape. You are now ready to write your speech.

THE OPENING LINE

This is an important part of your speech which many people overlook. It establishes your style and introduces you to everyone in the room. Example opening lines are included later in the book.

You may begin by thanking the previous speaker. This immediately creates a good flow and allows you to begin your

~ To flow smoothly the content of the speech must be arranged in a logical order.
A warm opening line, a good strong body, and a terrific ending. ~

16

◆

speech on a positive note.

A Good Strong Body

The body of your speech must really be decided by the content you have written.

Try to begin with the more serious aspects of your speech.

Build the speech to a humorous crescendo, including your jokes and funny stories.

As the laughter finally diminishes, wrap up the speech with a good sincere ending.

Know Your Ending

A good ending usually has a sincere ring of emotion.

You may be required to end your speech with the appropriate toast or make reference to the next speaker.

Refer to, *Traditional Order of Toasts and Speeches,* which outlines all the relevant toasts.

The sample speeches provided in this book include a range of excellent endings that are simple to use, to the point and effective.

Notes

DELIVERING YOUR SPEECH

♦

THE COMMON FEAR OF PUBLIC SPEAKING

Some lucky individuals have a natural gift when it comes to public speaking. They feel little nervousness at the prospect of facing a large audience.

If you are like most people, you will be nervous and perhaps a little frantic. You may even suffer some symptoms of fear.

By understanding what you may experience, you will come a long way towards solving the problem.

Public speaking is an unusual experience for most of us. We see the situation as threatening and fear embarrassing ourselves.

We react in the same way as if facing any threat, experiencing what is known as the "fight or flight" syndrome.

Our bodies prepare us to either face the threat or flee swiftly away.

The physical manifestations of this are an increase in blood pressure, pulse rate, and perspiration. Breathing may become irregular. You may become much more alert. Other

> *~ Like most people you may be nervous and perhaps a little frantic. ~*

18

symptoms include trembling hands and knees, stomach cramps, nausea, a dry mouth and butterflies in the stomach. Although unpleasant, all of these reactions are completely normal. Most public speakers experience them to some degree.

The more you are drawn upon to speak in public the less nervousness you will experience.

The only way to successfully master public speaking for the first time is to practise at home.

ALLOW TIME TO PRACTISE

You should begin at least three weeks before the wedding, if this is possible. If not, practise several times a day for as many days as you can find. Try to practise a few times in front of people who are not attending the wedding. They will give you an objective idea of how the speech sounds.

Before practising your speech out loud, sit quietly and read it through many times. Read it out loud, picking up any mistakes and correcting them. Ensure the speech flows well and words run together easily when spoken. Read and re-read until you automatically know what comes next. The more familiar you are with your speech the easier it will be to deliver.

SELECT THE MAIN POINTS OF THE SPEECH

Begin with your opening line and using a highlighting marker, select

~ *The more familiar you are with your speech the easier it will be to deliver.* ~

and highlight just the main points of each sentence. Be careful not to miss a main point or change in content. Forget all the miscellaneous wording which gives the speech flow. You are looking for specific pointers that will remind you of where you are up to in the speech.

Write them down on a separate piece of paper and check to make sure you have not forgotten anything.

Now you are ready for the most important part of your speech preparation and delivery.

NOTE CARDS

Many people feel they can memorise their speech and come out and perform without any notes.

More times than not, these are the people that become unstuck. Giving a speech is not a test of your

memory. People expect speakers to have notes. In fact, an audience finds it easier to listen to a speaker who occasionally looks down at his or her notes, than one who hits them with a continual flow of memorised words.

Note cards also allow you those all-important pauses, which are a chance to catch your breath and gather your thoughts.

Note cards should be small pieces of thick cardboard with very big, black letters outlining the main points within the speech.

Ensure you do not use flimsy paper. It will be hard to hold and if you are a little nervous and your

~ Giving a speech is not a test of your memory so do use notecards. ~

♦

hands shake, the paper will shake even more violently, accentuating your nervousness.

Using a perforator, place a hole in each card at the top left or right-hand corner, as you prefer.

Put the cards in order and number each note card with large figures.

Attach all the cards together with a key ring style attachment.

The cards, ring binder and thick black pen can all be purchased at your local newsagent or most supermarkets.

You can, of course, make your own cards with thick cardboard.

Write only a few different points on each card. Do not forget to note any anecdotes, quotes or jokes.

Ensure your note cards fit easily into a suit pocket (for male speakers) or handbag (for female speakers). And do not forget to take them with you on the day.

BEGIN AUDIBLE PRACTISE

Now you are completely ready to begin practising out loud. Stand in front of a mirror and, using your note cards, say your speech to yourself many times. Check the way you are standing. Stand tall but in a relaxed manner.

BEING HEARD

It may be difficult to judge whether or not you are speaking loud enough in the privacy of your home. You should never have to shout to be heard.

If the reception room is very large, then usually a microphone will be provided for your comfort.

~ Do not forget to take your note cards on the wedding day. ~

A good, strong, clear voice is the best guide. Try not to mumble your words or run sentences together.

Be prepared for laughter after the funny lines in your speech and allow a brief pause.

Keep your head well up and do not speak to the floor. Alternatively, do not speak to the ceiling.

Try not to speak to every person in the room. This will distract you, making your speech appear disjointed.

Actors are very experienced at a technique which involves selecting three people in the room at various positions; one to the front, the other two towards the rear of the room, at left and right positions.

Talk in the general direction of these three people and it will appear that you are speaking to the whole audience.

Obviously you may also look at specific people mentioned in the speech, for example: the mother of the bride, the father of the bride, grandparents, etc.

Another trick is to focus your attention just above the eyes of the audience. Glance towards their foreheads and you will be less likely to be distracted by a room full of people, all focusing their attention on you.

SOME DO'S AND DON'TS

Try not to focus on your notes too much. A brief glance should help you find your way.

Do not make them a crutch to hide any nervousness.

~ Be prepared for laughter after the funny lines in your speech. ~

♦

You should know your speech well enough by the day of the wedding. They are there to assist you, not to become the speech itself.

Try not to fidget too much. Practise relaxation techniques before the wedding day. Keep your inner-self calm and composed. Practise a relaxed stance in front of the mirror.

Try not to use words like "Ugh", "but", and "and" between sentences or as pauses. They are very distracting and sound unprofessional.

The very well prepared person who takes his or her role seriously has one last trick that can help make the speech even better:

RECORD YOUR SPEECH USING EITHER VIDEO OR AUDIO EQUIPMENT

If you have a video recorder, you may like to video your speech at home beforehand, wearing the outfit you will wear on the wedding day.

You can then check not only how the speech sounds, your pitch and level of volume, but also how you are visually presenting the speech.

Do not be overly critical, check for obvious problems, streamline your performance then relax and be confident in the knowledge that you have done your best!

This same technique is also possible using a tape recorder. Although you cannot see yourself, you

~ Record your speech using either video or audio equipment. ~

♦

can still check all details of how your speech sounds.

A FEW TIPS IF YOU ARE TO USE A MICROPHONE

It may be a good idea to inquire if you are to use a microphone on the wedding day.

Do not be nervous as it may greatly aid you on the day, enabling you to speak at your normal volume, therefore eliminating the need to speak loudly to the back of the room.

When you arrive at the reception take a brief moment to check if the microphone can be heightened or lowered to suit yourself.

Check how it operates and give it a quick test, if possible. Adjusting the microphone to the correct position will enable you to stand in a relaxed manner.

When first speaking into the microphone, talk softly until you get used to the volume level and then raise your voice carefully to an audible level.

If you are to be the first speaker it may be a good idea to say briefly: "I'm just checking the microphone. Can you all hear me to the rear of the room". This can break the ice and also help you feel more comfortable as the first speaker.

Do not speak into the microphone too closely as the sound system will tend to pick up your breathing as well. Alternatively, do not stand too far away.

Do not sway from side to

~ A microphone can be an added bonus, eliminating the need to shout to the back of the room. ~

side, as this can give an "up and down" effect to the volume level.

Do not hunch over the microphone. It is not necessary and will make you appear awkward.

Stand calmly in your usual relaxed manner about fifteen centimetres away and everything will flow smoothly.

A DRESS REHEARSAL

Most reception venues will not mind if you have a rehearsal at their venue before the wedding day. This is not a necessity, but if possible and convenient, will aid your confidence.

You do not have to perform your whole speech at the venue. Just seeing the layout of the room and where you are to stand can help greatly.

FINAL TIPS FOR GOOD SPEECH DELIVERY

Do not race through the speech. It will appear as though you cannot wait to finish and you are not enjoying the experience. Alternatively, do not speak so slowly that people feel as though they want to fill in the words for you or hit you over the back to get on with things.

Do not deliver the speech using only one tone of voice. A long monologue of words will sound very negative if you do not vary your voice. Vary the emotional emphasis and your speech will hold the listeners' interest.

Do not worry if you find yourself lost in the middle

~ Most reception venues will make their premises available for a rehearsal before the wedding day. ~

of the speech and suddenly feel very nervous. Simply take a sip of water from a glass, which is usually provided for speakers at weddings, take a look at your notes, then casually begin again. People will think this appears perfectly natural. Be aware of who is to speak before or after you. Will there be a Master of Ceremonies who will make the various introductions, or do you have to do this for the speaker after you?

Introduce yourself to the Master of Ceremonies if you have not met before the wedding, as this will greatly ease their role of introducing you.

THE MOST IMPORTANT RULE OF ALL

Relax! This is not an inquisition, it is a wedding, one of the most joyous and beautiful celebrations of life. If you look forward to the event and think of it as a happy occasion, you will undoubtedly perform well!

NOTES

ON THE DAY

♦

Well, here it is. The big day has arrived, you have practised for weeks, you are well prepared and feeling rather confident. So far, so good.

Before you leave for the wedding ensure you have your notes tucked snugly into a pocket or your handbag, whatever the case may be.

Check your clothing and appearance. If you feel confident about how you look then you will project this to your audience.

It is a good idea to carry some tissues or a handkerchief to avoid embarrassment if you suddenly have an attack of sneezes during your speech.

Try not to dwell on your speech during the ceremony. Forget about it and enjoy yourself.

AT THE RECEPTION

You will not be called upon to speak until after dinner is finished, so relax and enjoy yourself.

Do not dwell on the speech during dinner.

Once the last course is completed it is nearly time for the speeches to begin.

This can be the time when many speakers find themselves feeling

~ You will not be called on to speak until after dinner. ~

nervous. If this happens to you, make an effort to relax yourself both physically and mentally. Relax yourself in the chair. If you sit as tight as a rock you will worsen the whole experience.

If someone is speaking before you, really listen to their speech. This will take your mind off your own and help you to relax.

If nerves are getting the better of you, begin deep breathing relaxation techniques. Breath deeply and relax your whole body. Sip an alcoholic beverage to help you relax. But do not consume too much, or the alcohol will hit you suddenly and you may feel quite ill.

THE TIME HAS COME

The time has come to give your speech and the most important thing to remember is - Be there! There is nothing worse than a speaker who has disappeared to the bathroom, or outside for a breath of fresh air at the vital moment.

Make all your movements a little slower than usual, this will help you to relax. Many speakers have the tendency to speed up a little, their nervousness causing this effect. This is when accidents are most likely to happen and you do not want to make a grand entrance by tripping over your chair.

Take things slowly and deliberately and you will do just fine.

TIME FOR YOUR NOTE CARDS

Take your notes out and

~ When the time comes for your speech make sure you are there! ~

28

◆

have them ready in your hands.

You will need a glass of wine or champagne if you are to propose a toast, so ensure this is available.

You may have been provided with a glass of water for your convenience.

Try to stand calmly. Do not jingle keys in your pocket, scratch your nose, or hop from foot to foot.

Be prepared for the audience to make some light-hearted remarks during your speech. Do not get annoyed by this. Laugh with them, then return to your speech.

If you are quick-witted you may like to respond to the remarks.

Be prepared for anything that may go wrong. For example, the lights suddenly going out, a tray of glasses being dropped, or the microphone suddenly dying.

Things like this are inevitable in life, so do not get too concerned if they happen to you.

If all else fails and something does go wrong, just react with humour and a sense of fun. The guests will enjoy your spontaneity and humour.

Finally, remember this is a wedding and the guests are eagerly looking forward to your speech.

Relax and enjoy your contribution to one of life's great occasions.

~ Remember, the guests are looking forward to hearing the speeches. Relax, and enjoy your contribution to one of life's great occasions. ~

OPENING LINES FOR YOUR SPEECH

♦

The following opening lines for your speech are readymade introductions that require no further embellishment.

The most frequently used traditional opening line for a wedding speech is:

Ladies and gentlemen....

This can be extended for very formal weddings to:

Ladies, gentlemen and honoured guests...

For informal or intimate weddings a suitable opening would be:

Dear friends...

FATHER OF THE BRIDE

SINCERE

It is with the greatest of pleasure that I speak to you today.
If my smile from ear to ear gives me away, then I hope these words express some of my excitement and joy...

It is my very pleasant duty to welcome you all to Kate and Peter's wedding...

My wife, Margaret, and I are truly delighted that you could share this wonderful day with us...

This is an important day for us all but not quite so

important as for the wonderful couple on my right. I was privileged to be the father of one at the beginning of the day and now I stand as the proud father of two. And what a "two" they are...

HUMOROUS

Before all else I just want to stand here in front of you and take a moment of your time - to gloat!

(*Pause for at least ten seconds, exaggerate your stance with chest out and a big smile.*)

At the end of this day I will have lost two very important things.. a wonderful daughter (*pause*) and my life savings! No, no, I'm only joking. As you can see, I still have my daughter...

Today I thought to myself, `I'm not nervous' But after I put my shoes on the wrong feet, my shirt on inside out and drove to the wrong church I realised, forget it, everyone will know you're nervous. But to cap it all off I brought the wrong speech, so I hope you don't mind if I talk to you today about... fishing. No seriously...

My wife, Margaret has thought of everything for me today. She organised my suit, a hair cut and a shoe polish. She woke me up, ensured I had my notes for this speech, and even told me when to stand up a moment ago. But sure enough there was one thing she should have known I would've needed. A big box of tissues at the ceremony. I didn't think I would shed a tear, but alas, I shed many...

31

GROOM

SINCERE

Surrounded by so many of our closest friends and relatives, this speech is not a duty, it is a pleasure...

I would like to begin by thanking Kate's father, John, for his kind words...

Today you are looking at the happiest man alive and it is my great privilege to stand here and express my sincere thanks to...

Your being here today is the first great achievement of our marriage and I thank you all for coming here to celebrate our wedding day...

HUMOROUS

Since I first saw Kate I haven't been able to take my eyes off her. I'm sure you won't mind if I speak to you... but look at her. (*Stand facing the bride, preferably with your back to the audience.*)

Firstly I would like to thank Kate's father for his kind words and say, `Ha, you can't tell her what to do anymore!'

BEST MAN

SINCERE

When (*groom*) asked me to be his Best Man, all I could think about was the opportunity of being able to tell you all what a really great mate he has been...

These beautiful ladies (*gesture towards the bridesmaids*) who have helped to make this day truly special have asked me to acknowledge your best wishes, compliments and gratitude...

HUMOROUS

If I'm the Best Man, how come Peter gets to go home with Kate and I go home alone to my dog. Well, I'll just have to work on the bridesmaids, who I'm sure you will agree look stunning.

If I'm the Best Man why isn't the bride marrying me?...

I'm afraid that the term "Best Man" creates unrealistic expectations to be the "best" organised, "best" dressed, "best" looking, etc. Although I can fill all those roles, I do not think I can give the "best" speech. How could I upstage Kate's father, or for that matter, Peter's.

BRIDE

SINCERE

I knew that I couldn't be here today without taking this opportunity to say thank you to my wonderful parents who have made all this possible.

It is with the greatest pleasure that I welcome you to the celebration of our marriage.

Being a modern girl, I couldn't let this opportunity slip by without saying a few words of welcome and gratitude to you all, for helping make this special day complete.

HUMOROUS

They say that second thoughts are always best. Well, when God first

◆

created man, woman was his second thought. Now with this in mind, I thought it was definitely my right to say a few words....

At most weddings, the father of the bride speaks, the groom speaks and the best man speaks. All men! Hey, isn't this a bit sexist. Well I'm here tonight to help even the score...

To break with tradition I refused to say: `Love, honour and "OBEY"', I didn't wear a white dress and I'm definitely not going to keep quiet at the reception. As a modern girl, I just wanted to take this opportunity to welcome you all here today...

NOTES

POPULAR QUOTATIONS

ABSENCE

Absence makes the heart grow fonder.
Thomas Taynes Bayly, Isle of Beauty.

Say, is not absence death to those who love?
Alexander Pope, Autumn

BEAUTY

A thing of beauty is a joy forever; its loveliness increases; it will never pass into nothingness.
John Keats, Endymion

If eyes were made for seeing, then beauty is its own excuse for being.
Ralph Waldo Emerson, The Rhodora

Beauty is in the eye of the beholder.

EYES

Her glance, how wildly beautiful. *Lord Byron*

Drink to me only with thine eyes, and I will pledge with mine;
Or leave a kiss within the

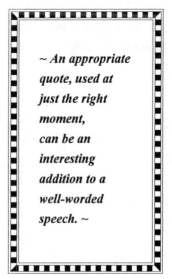

*~ An appropriate quote, used at just the right moment,
can be an interesting addition to a well-worded speech. ~*

◆

cup, and I'll not look for wine. *Ben Johnson*

FRIENDSHIP

The only way to have a friend is to be one.
Ralph Waldo Emerson

HAPPINESS

The foolish person seeks happiness in the distance, the wise grow it under their feet.
James Oppenheim

The grand essentials of happiness are something to do, something to love, and something to hope for.
Allan K. Chalmers

Happiness comes of the capacity to feel deeply, to enjoy simply, to think freely, to be needed.
Storm Jameson

KINDNESS

Kindness in words creates confidence, kindness in thinking creates profoundness, kindness in giving creates love. *Lao-tse*

LOVE

We can do no great things, only small things with great love.
Mother Teresa

In dreams and in love there are no impossibilities.
Janos Arany

We are all born for love. It is the principle of existence, and its only end.
Benjamin Disraeli, Sibyl

Two souls with but a single thought, two hearts that beat as one.
*Friedrich Halm,
Ingomar the Barbarian*

◆

Treasure the love you receive above all. It will survive long after your gold and good health have vanished. *Og Mandino*

You will find as you look back upon your life that the moments when you have really lived, are the moments when you have done things in the spirit of love.
Henry Drummond

Love is everything. It is the key to life, and its influences are those that move the world.
Ralph Waldo Trine

MARRIAGE

Marriages are made in Heaven. *Proverb*

Marriage has many pains, but celibacy has no pleasures.
Samuel Johnson, Rasselas

Marriage is popular because it combines the maximum of temptation with the maximum of opportunity.
George Bernard Shaw

MEN AND WOMEN

Men have sight, women insight.
Victor Hugo

PEACE

Peace cannot be kept by force. It can only be achieved by understanding.
Albert Einstein

TRUTH

Truth is the property of no individual, but is the treasure of all.
Ralph Waldo Emerson

WEDDING JOKES

♦

Humour is the highlight of any good wedding speech. Ensure that the audience will understand any jokes included, and that all humour is in good taste.

If I am supposed to be the "Best Man', then why has *(Bride's name)* married *(Groom's name)*.

How come *(Groom's name)* is more nervous about his wedding speech, than his wedding night.

I'd like to take this opportunity to thank the two most important guests who have made this wedding possible. Could you all please raise your glasses...To American Express and Visa, without who we could not be here today.

The bride's parents should always remember, they haven't lost a daughter, just gained another problem.

Groucho Marx once said, "Marriage is an institution. But who wants to live in an institution."

Marriage is a case of give and take. You give and she takes.

The bride's mother always thinks of everything. Everything, that is, except a box of tissues.

I'll never forget the night I proposed to my wife, or

the words I said "you're not, are you?"

Recently, a 90 year old man got married. You won't believe it but the girl was only 18. The doctor warned him that this arrangement could be very bad for the heart. The old man replied "Well, if she dies, she dies.."

I was told the other day that a wedding is much like a funeral. Everyone cries and your life is over.

Most men are surprised when they see the marriage certificate. There's no expiry date!

I'm sorry if I embarrassed anyone during the photo session. How was I to know what the photographer meant, when he said, "A quick flash of the Best Man!".

At the last wedding that I attended, when a woman in my pew went to communion she trod right on my foot.
When she returned she said to me, "Did I tread on your foot?" thinking she was going to apologise, I said, "Well, yes, actually you did".
To my surprise she replied, "Good then this is my row."

NOTES

THE SPEECHES

When reading the following speeches it is important to remember that no individual speech can give you every detail you will need for yours. This would be impossible. The speeches presented here give you many ideas to work with.

When adapted they could become the skeleton of your speech.

The content may be adjusted to suit your particular circumstances or you may decide to choose some lines from each and design your own individual speech accordingly.

Humour is a very difficult thing to write in a generalised way.

Humour is a personal thing and should be adapted to suit your particular situation.

With this in mind the speeches presented here are light-hearted, but remain basically sincere.

You may wish to include further stories, anecdotes or jokes that take your fancy and will be easily understood by your particular audience.

The variety and length of the various speeches should enable you to extend them easily.

You may decide to keep your speech short and succinct.

This is a good idea if you are particularly nervous. In this case, your speech should remain sincere and serious, as this will have

more impact.
Some of the speeches
include quotes and poems
to show you how these
may be used effectively.
No one can know the
circumstances of your
wedding so do try to
personalise any speech
you may use.
The speech you deliver
should reflect the
individuality of the
wedding you are to attend.

FATHER OF THE BRIDE

It is the Father of the
Bride's privilege to deliver
the first speech at the
wedding reception and he
usually begins by
welcoming all guests.
Guests delight in this
speech and it sets the tone
for the proceedings.
Further to his own speech,
it is delightful when the
Father of the Bride calls
the Mother of the Bride
forth to say a few words in
her own right.
The Father of the Bride
concludes by offering the
official toast: "To the
health and happiness of
the Bride and Groom."

SPEECH 1

Ladies and gentlemen,
My wife and I have spent
the past (*number*)
months/years observing a
very special relationship
develop.
At first, not taking it
terribly seriously, but
before long, seeing it
blossom into something
substantial and intense.
It became obvious that a
certain young couple were
quite serious about each
other.
This relationship has led
us to this very important
and happy day.

In thinking about what I should say and what was really important to the whole proceedings, I sat with our guest list in front of me, thinking about the two wonderful newly-weds and now, glancing around the room, I know I have chosen the right topic...friendship.

I looked up the meaning of friendship in the dictionary. Stated simply; it is the feeling that subsists between friends or binds them to one another; a kind regard invoking respect and intimacy.

It was these feelings that brought (*Bride's name*) mother, (*Mother's name*), and myself together so many years ago, and throughout our marriage we have never lost sight of the true friendship that we are blessed to enjoy.

It was a simple friendship that drew (*Bride*) and (*Groom*) together, a friendship that developed into a special love they have today celebrated by publicly joining together in the bond of marriage.

I am honoured to speak to a room filled with our dearest friends who have shared so much of our lives over the years.

Friendship is the basis of all good relationships. A friend is someone you care about, respect and look after. You look forward to seeing a friend. You worry about them and try to help when things go wrong.

Marriage is all about such friendship and in the words of Ralph Waldo Emerson, "the only way to have a friend, is to be one".

If (*Bride*) and (*Groom*) can always remember the friendship that they started their relationship with, strive to preserve and improve it, loving each other with respect and

♦

honesty, then theirs will be a long and happy union.

I want to thank you all for being here today and celebrating (*Bride*) and (*Groom's*) wedding vows. (*Bride*) has given her parents a life time of joy and laughter over the years and it is with a potent mix of melancholy and happiness that we see her embark on a new life with (*Groom*) today.

We have been delighted to come to know (*Groom's*) family. They have added an exciting new dimension to our lives.

There is such empathy between the two families that it is a further joy to look forward to a future of wonderful social occasions. Well, any excuse will do! (*Wry grin*). It is now my very pleasant duty to ask all of our dearest friends here today to please stand and raise your glasses.

Join with me now to wish (*Bride*) and (*Groom*) all the best of health and happiness as they begin their life journey together as husband and wife...

To (*Bride*) and (*Groom*)...

SPEECH 2

Ladies and Gentlemen, It is my very pleasant duty to welcome you all here today to celebrate the marriage of (*Bride*) and (*Groom*).

I know that many of our guests have travelled quite a distance to be here and it is with a special thank you that we welcome you all to this happy occasion.

As I look around the room I realise what good and dear friends we are so fortunate to have.

This wedding has brought us all together and we hope you have a really wonderful time this evening.

I am extremely proud to have the opportunity of saying a few words of welcome.

I'm sure you will agree that this is one of the most beautiful weddings in the world. I'm sure you won't mind if I boast a little. (*Bride*) looks magnificent and (*Groom*) looks well, OK. No, no, I mean, handsome.

I cannot let him get away with too much or my father-in-law lectures will not hold much strength in the future.

As I watched (*Bride*) take her wedding vows I marveled at the controlled, elegant woman before me. It was with a tear in my eye that I thought back to a day, many years ago, when I heard the words "You have a beautiful, baby girl". She screamed so loudly at the hospital that I thought it MUST be a boy, and a whole football team, at that!

She was a very determined person from the moment she took her first breath, and it is the same determination, which I might add was inherited from her mother, that has seen them both plan and execute this magnificent event today.

If she is head strong, then she has met her match with (*Groom*). Theirs will be a union of equals, which I know will ensure that they carve an exciting, rewarding, road together.

It was obvious from meeting (*Groom's*) family that he is a man of honesty, loyalty and integrity.

It has been such an honour to celebrate this magnificent event with a family such as his.

My wife, (*Name*), has been a real pillar of strength over the past few weeks.

My nervousness was always abated by her cool, calm, patient nature. In my life she has made me the happiest man alive and I must take this opportunity to thank her for her enduring love. When I reflect over our many wonderful married years I envy (*Bride*) and (*Groom's*) youth, as they embark on an exciting journey through life together.

It is now my very great privilege to ask you to propose a toast to my daughter and son-in-law. Could you all please stand and with all the very best wishes, raise your glasses to (*Bride*) and (*Groom*), as we wish them the greatest health and happiness for their future life together.

To (Bride) and (Groom)....

SPEECH 3

Note: When reciting the poem below during your speech, deliberately speak slowly, with definite pauses between each line. You must emphasise that you are reciting a poem, so people can hear you well and clearly understand each line.

Ladies and gentlemen, A great poet, Kahlil Gibran, wrote a beautiful poem about marriage that encapsulates everything I could wish to say today. I hope you do not mind if I share it with you now... Ay, you shall be together even in the silent memory of God. But let there be spaces in your togetherness and let the winds of the heavens dance between you. Love one another but make not a bond of love. Let it rather be a moving

sea, between the shores
of your souls.
Fill each other's cup
but drink not from the
same cup.
Give one another of your
bread but eat not from the
same loaf.
Sing and dance together
and be joyous, but let each
one of you be alone.
Even as the strings of a
lute are alone though they
quiver with the same
music.
Give your hearts, but not
into each other's keeping.
For only the hand of life
can contain your hearts.
And stand together yet not
too near together.
For the pillars of the
temple stand apart,
And the oak tree and the
cypress grow not in each
other's shadow...
These are the words that
really express everything
that I wanted to say.
(*Bride*) and (*Groom*) stand
today as two unique

individuals.
They have come from very
different backgrounds and
circumstances.
They are both strong-
minded and determined.
They are attractive, young,
with the promise of a
wonderful life ahead.
It is my very sincere hope
that as they grow in life
together, they always
remember and respect
each other's individuality,
as we have honoured the
joining of two such
individuals today.
I would also like to take
this opportunity to thank
all of our oldest and
dearest friends for joining
us in celebration of this
wonderful wedding.
My wife (*Wife's name*)
and I are sad to lose the
daughter who has filled
our home with so much
happiness over the years,
but we look forward to
many years enjoying the
company of (*Bride*) and

(*Groom*) together.

It is now a pleasure and a privilege to ask you all to be upstanding.

To (*Bride*) and (*Groom*), may your future be filled with the greatest blessings and joys that life may bestow upon you.

May you enjoy many years of prosperity and good health.

May your individuality bring strength to your union.

We wish you all the best that life has to offer...

To (*Bride*) and (*Groom*)...

SPEECH 4

Ladies and Gentlemen, Thank you for joining us today for what is a memorable occasion for my family, and I'm sure (*Groom's*) family.

This day celebrates the beginning of a wonderful new phase in our lives.

Perhaps the wisest thing anyone has ever said to me about marriage and love is this: love is a decision.

On the surface, its sounds like a fairly clinical and unromantic assessment.

But think about it a little deeper and you will realise the truth that rings out in those words.

You see, it's easy to fall in love. When a young couple first meet the world looks rosy, neither can do any wrong, nothing can touch them.

But as you grow into your relationship and the realities of life take hold - things like a mortgage, kids, joys, sufferings, general ups and downs - you start to realise that real love is a conscious decision.

Relationships take a lot of work. You have to be working at them all the time so that you grow together.

♦

When you hit a bump, that's the time to stop and say: "Love is a decision. I made a conscious decision to love this man, or woman, despite his or her shortfalls, despite my not agreeing with everything he or she says and does. Because I love this person, I can resolve any problem we might face."

If you look at love in this way, then nothing can stop you.

(*Bride*) and (*Groom*) are sensible enough to see the reason in what I'm saying - (*Bride*) because she's my daughter and (*Groom*) because he wants to stay my son-in-law.

To all our friends and family, thank you for being here to share this day with us.

I'm sure (*Bride*) and (*Groom*) are heartened and strengthened by your goodwill.

Thank you all for being so attentive.

I cannot recall (*Bride*) and (*Groom*) listening to me so intently since that night when they sat nervously on the couch waiting for my reaction to the news of their plans to marry.

Well, I'm glad I said yes and I'm glad to be here tonight to tell you so.

So let's raise our glasses and wish a lifetime of happiness to ...

(*Bride*) and (*Groom*).

SPEECH 5

Ladies and gentlemen,

When (*Bride*) stood at the alter earlier today and spoke those magic words, "I Do", I had cause to reflect that it's one of the few times in her life she's agreed to do something without question.

That's not to say (*Bride*) was disobedient as a child, or in any way a trouble-maker. But she's always

♦

been headstrong - as many of you know and as (*Groom*) is finding out. In fact, I have a feeling that what she really wanted to say today was "I do as I please".

Well, (*Groom*), I can see that she's very pleased to be marrying you - just as (*Wife*) and I are pleased to welcome you into our family.

Over the time we've known you, (*Wife*) and I have noticed many things about you - most of which I'd rather not repeat in mixed company.

But the thing that stands out is the love that you obviously feel for (*Bride*). As a father, I could not ask for any more from a prospective son-in-law. And so I now entrust her to you, safe in the knowledge that she is with a man who loves and respects her just as she loves and respects him.

A marriage is a joining of two individuals. Although (*Bride and Groom's*) lives are now symbolically one, it's important that each of you realise that your partner is his or her own person. Come to understand and appreciate your differences. If you do, your relationship will grow in trust and mutual respect - and you will then appreciate how much you really do have in common.

Let me now thank all of you for coming here today to share our joy.

Some of you have travelled far to be here and we are honoured by your presence. I am sure you will agree the beautiful spectacle of (*Bride and Groom's*) coming together makes it all worthwhile.

And so I would now ask you to raise your glasses, and join me in a toast...to (*Bride and Groom*).

SPEECH 6

Ladies and gentlemen,
You will forgive me
tonight if I seem a little
emotional. I can assure
you it's nothing to do with
the cost of this wedding.
It's not everyday that I
give away a daughter -
although there's probably
been many times in the
past when I've very much
wanted to.

Today, however, I've done
it with great reluctance.
Not that I hold any grudge
with (*Groom*). He is an
impressive young man, a
credit to his family and an
asset to mine.

But in seeing (*Bride*) to
the altar today, I was
struck with a realisation
that an important phase in
our lives has come and
gone.

My little girl has grown
up, left home and gotten
married. When I look back
over the years, I realise

now how little time you
really do have with your
children.

For the first ten years or
so, they are totally reliant
on you. Then, as they gain
independence, the roles
reverse. You follow in
their footsteps, trying to
keep up with them.

I am grateful for the
precious relationship I've
shared with my daughter.
Now I share her with
(*Groom*). The consolation
is that he obviously loves
her as much as I do. That
makes it easier for me to
stand up here tonight.

(*Bride*), I could not be any
prouder of you. You are a
beautiful young woman.
You have already achieved
a lot in your young life,
and I know you will
achieve a lot more.

Your mother and I wish
you and (*Groom*) all the
happiness and prosperity
in the world.

Know that you will face

many ups and downs in your married life, but know too that if you truly love each other you will grow and prosper together. Thank you to everyone of our friends and family who are with us today. This is a family celebration, and it is enlivened by your presence here.

I would now ask you to raise your glasses and join me in a toast to the future health and happiness of the Bride and Groom.

...to (*Bride and Groom.*)

BRIDE & GROOM

It is important to remember that it is the groom's duty to thank everyone concerned with the wedding.

Remember to thank the following people:

- ◆ Bride
- ◆ Father of the Bride
- ◆ Mother of the Bride
- ◆ Groom's parents
- ◆ Best Man
- ◆ Groomsmen
- ◆ Bridesmaids
- ◆ Ushers
- ◆ Officiator
- ◆ Relatives
- ◆ Friends

The groom should not worry if his speech is not full of jokes and humour. People expect him to remain sincere and appreciative of the wedding.

Any humour included should be used tactfully and in good taste.

The guests traditionally enjoy the groom's speech if it includes lots of attention to the bride. After all, they are there to celebrate the marriage of the bride and groom. People will appreciate

your sense of romance!
If you wish to keep your speech short and succinct, then a general "thank you" to all concerned with the wedding will suffice.

Within this section we have also included two speeches specifically for the bride.

She may decide to begin her speech during the groom's speech as our first example shows, or a more appropriate time may be scheduled.
It is a wonderful addition to the modern wedding to hear the bride speak!

SPEECH 1

Ladies and gentlemen,
This has been a really wonderful day and it is my very great privilege to thank everyone for helping (*Bride*) and I celebrate our marriage.
How can I begin to express our gratitude to

(*Mother of the Bride and Father of the Bride*) for their enormous generosity in providing such a magnificent event.

In the (*months/years*) that I have come to know (*Bride's*) family, I have always sensed a great deal of friendship and hospitality.

This is reflected in their many wonderful friends I am having the pleasure of meeting today.

My family has given us a great deal of support also and I am honoured to thank them for their kindness. Ours has always been a happy home and I shall miss them very much.

(*Bride*) and I would like to thank everyone for the presents we have received. They will all help to make our life more enjoyable as we establish a new home together.

I would also like to thank

everyone who has contributed to make this day extra special. Our wonderful ushers were marvellous at the church and surely helped the ceremony flow smoothly. I'm sure you will agree that this wedding has a fantastic atmosphere. This has been created by the endless attention to every detail so skillfully executed by (*Bride*) and (*Bride's Mother*). I must say that I have not had to think of a thing.

I am the luckiest man alive today and to let you all further relish (*Bride's*) company, it is my pleasure to call upon (*Bride*) to say a few words. Any excuse to have her by my side... (*Stretch out your hand, indicating for the bride to join you.*)

Thank you (*Groom*), Ladies and gentlemen, I wanted to say a few words today as I could not let this opportunity pass.

My first very special thank you must be to my wonderful parents. The support, encouragement and love that they have shown me over the years has been enormous. They taught me to believe in myself and that anything that I wanted to do in life, I could do, if I just put my mind to it.

I was given a fantastic education and they have instilled in me values that I hope to bring to my marriage with (*Groom*). I am going to miss Mum and Dad's home very much but hope to create the same feeling of welcome and happiness in our new home.

It is difficult to express the gratitude that I have for this wonderful wedding. So much time and effort has gone into every detail.

My parents have truly provided the wedding of my dreams and it is with only wonderful memories that I will think of this day forever.

My bridesmaids have given me so much support and friendship over the last few months. All those secrets about the wedding that I could not tell (*Groom*), and all the "girls' talk" late into the evening that exhausted me so much. It was wonderful. They look so beautiful today, as do the groomsmen. If I wasn't here to marry (*Groom*) I definitely would have raced one of them away tonight.

I could not end without saying what a wonderful family (*Groom*) has. They have always made me feel welcome in their home and I feel that being with them is like an extension of my own family.

I look forward to all the future years we will have to enjoy and I thank them for the endless contributions they have made to this wedding.

Finally, I just want to say how enormously lucky I feel that life has brought (*Groom*) and I together. (*Taking Groom by the hand*) He is my best friend and greatest ally. I am so proud to be joined in marriage with a person to whom I feel such respect, love and admiration.

Thank you all for coming and I look forward to seeing such dear friends in our new home in the not too distant future.

(*Groom finalises his speech now and proposes the traditional toast to the bridesmaids.*)

Well I'm sure you all now know why I am the luckiest man alive. (*Bride*) and I will never forget this day or the kind wishes

♦

from all our friends.
The groomsmen here have done everything possible to get rid of me so they could stand in and marry (*Bride*).

But I survived and can only thank them now for their support and encouragement. (*Said in a sarcastic tone of voice*).

No, I'm only joking, they were really great and a fantastic help over the last few months.

If (*Bride*) wants to run off with one of the groomsmen then she can. With such beautiful bridesmaids I'm sure I can turn my attention elsewhere.

I know their support to (*Bride*) has been unceasing. Every time I went near (*Bride*) they were either hiding her from me or pushing me out of the room. Thank God they're not coming on the honeymoon! They're

not are they (*Bride*)? (*Turn to bride with a look of despair on your face*). Well if they have to come at least they are the most beautiful bridesmaids I have ever seen.

It is with thanks and gratitude in mind that I ask you all now to stand and join with me to express our appreciation to our bridesmaids.
To the bridesmaids.....

SPEECH 2

Ladies and Gentlemen,
It will be difficult to speak after (*Bride's Father's*) kind words. It is only with the greatest admiration that I can reply. (*Bride's*) family have truly become my own in the last two years and I am the luckiest man alive to be a part of such a wonderful clan.
My family has given me a great life up to now, and I will miss them very much.

(*Bride and I*) will endeavour to recreate the warmth and hospitality in our own home and enjoy the same happiness within marriage that our parents have experienced.

This wedding is the culmination of many brilliant organisational talents.

It goes without saying that (*Bride*) and (*Bride's Mother*) have created a magnificent event.

Their endless attention to every detail has ensured that we can all enjoy this splendid day in comfort and style.

I must say that our back-up team has been fantastic.

The bridesmaids and groomsmen have contributed enormous time and effort.

The ushers at the church performed brilliantly and the many friends and relatives who have helped in so many ways deserve special thanks.

(*Bride*) and I would also like to thank everyone for the wonderful presents we have received.

You have really been too generous and I know that we shall always remember each and everyone of you through the many useful things we now have to help establish our home.

Every groom has a Best Man and undoubtedly I have the "Best", Best Man.

(*Best Man*) has been a very good friend and a real tower of strength as I nervously approached the big day.

I now have a most pleasurable duty to perform.

It is with special thanks to our magnificent bridesmaids that I ask you all to be upstanding and join with me to toast these beautiful, wonderful, ladies...

To the bridesmaids...

SPEECH 3

Ladies and gentlemen,
Firstly, I would like to thank (*Bride's Father*) for his kind words.

I hold enormous admiration for a man who helped bring into the world, the wonderful girl I have just married.

I thought I would fly by the seat of my pants for this speech and follow my heart, today.

Well the only emotion that I am feeling is overwhelming happiness.

It was Allan Chalmers who once said: "The grand essentials of happiness are something to do, something to love, and something to hope for".

My parents gave me a wonderful upbringing and education, and this has ensured that I have something to do, (*turning towards the bride*) I now have someone very special to love, and through our marriage today, I have a fantastic future to hope for.

If these are the essentials of happiness then I am the luckiest man alive.

This is truly the happiest day of my life and I cannot thank (*Bride's Mother and Father*) enough for this wonderful wedding.

It is with endless gratitude that we shall remember this day forever.

This thank you must also be extended to my own family. They have been wonderful and truly committed to the success of this day.

So many people have contributed so much time and effort. It is impossible to mention everyone individually so I just want to extend our most sincere thank you to everyone concerned.

There is one person though who I must

mention. My "Best" Man (*Best Man*) has ensured that I did not forget one detail.

All my duties have been attended to with the skill of a well-trained army.

He even saved my life at the "bucks night" and ensured that I made it here today in one piece.

I'm getting all this praise in early, as it is his turn to speak next and I do want (*Bride*) to talk to me on the honeymoon.

While I have the opportunity, do not believe a word he says, unless it is complimentary, of course.

Well, whatever he says I would not be telling the truth unless I expressed my overwhelming gratitude for his unflinching support in the line of duty.

It must be said that I had absolutely no idea of what (*Bride*) and her bridesmaids were going to look like today.

Over the last few months I heard many whispered words that had no need to be said in such lowered tones of voice. I had no idea what they meant anyway. Words like brocade, shantung, taffeta and organza were floated around with such authority that everyone seemed to automatically know their meaning. I thought they had developed a new language to fool me. Well, they succeeded in one thing, I did feel a fool.

That was until today. When those doors opened and (*Bride*) and her beautiful bridesmaids appeared, I thought I was in heaven and now understand why fabrics are given such exotic names. They looked magnificent!

I now fully appreciate the hours of endless help and detail that the bridesmaids gave to (*Bride*) over the

◆

last few months.
I want to take this opportunity to thank them all and it is my honoured duty to ask you to join with me now for this very special toast to these beautiful ladies..
Ladies and gentlemen, to the bridesmaids....

SPEECH 4

Ladies and gentlemen, I'm not sure who is happier tonight - (Bride), myself or my mother. (Bride) because she's got me, me because I've got her and mum because she's got a spare room.
No more washing and cleaning up after me, no more staying up worrying about what time I'm coming home. Now that responsibility's transferred to (Bride)! Only kidding, my darling.
Seriously, though, I would like to pay a tribute to

Mum and Dad and thank them for the great job they've done in raising me, guiding me and providing for me. I wouldn't be here tonight without them - ain't that the truth!
I know I speak for (Bride) when I say thank you to her parents for this evening, and for all the blessings they have bestowed on us in recent months.
Together, our two sets of parents are an inspiration. If our lives can mirror what they have achieved, then we'll be travelling very well indeed.
And if we can avoid all the bad habits that these fellows on my right demonstrate on a regular basis (point to Best Man and Groomsman), we'll be healthy, wealthy and wise! (Best Man) was telling me only today that he felt a great sense of responsibility towards me.

I know exactly what he means. After all, he's responsible for the terrible hangover I suffered after the buck's night. Having said that, though, I couldn't ask for better friends than (*Best Man and Groomsman*).

You do me great honour by being a part of this wedding and I sincerely thank you.

We've had many helpers today and in the past few months. To all of you, too many to mention individually, please accept our sincerest thanks.

I walked outside a few moments ago and thought it was Christmas. There are so many presents out there. Thank you everyone for your generosity.

I've not yet mentioned the most important person here tonight - my wife. It's not too often I get lost for words, but I did this afternoon when (*Bride*) started walking down the aisle towards me.

In hindsight, it's probably just as well because I wasn't supposed to say anything at that point anyway!

(*Bride*), you are the love of my life and I look forward to a happy, fulfilling and loving life together.

I have one last duty to perform before I sit down. On our left sit a posse of beautiful women - (*Bride's*) bridesmaids. Thank you for all your efforts today and over the past months.

I would now ask you to stand and join me in toasting these special ladies...to our bridesmaids.

SPEECH 5

Ladies and gentlemen, There are so many people to thank here tonight. I want to start with my wife. Standing in church today, I guess I was struck with the realisation of what marriage is really all about. It is a binding together of two people's lives, in every sense of the word.

I'm sure we'll know tough times as well as good times, but I'm equally confident that our mutual trust, respect and love will carry us over every hurdle.

(*Bride*) and I have entered into this marriage as best friends. I've never had a best friend like (*Bride*) before.

For a start, most of them have had considerably flatter chests and much deeper voices - like (*Best Man*) here.

But our friendship has proved to be a springboard from which we have grown together in love. I cannot describe in words what I feel for (*Bride*) tonight. I can only say that there is no prouder man in this room.

(*Bride's*) father might dispute me. He deserves to be proud.

To (*Bride's parents*), and to my parents, (*Groom's parents*), thanks for everything you have done for us, not just tonight but over our entire lives.

We can never repay you, except by following the examples you have each set us.

The celebration this evening is everything we could have wished for.

We are surrounded by family and good friends and we are sincerely moved by the expressions of goodwill from all of you.

Thank you, too, for your gifts. We appreciate your generosity.

To everyone else who played a role in today's event - from our ushers and celebrant right through to the musicians and staff here at the reception centre - a big thanks.

I cannot forget (*Best Man*) here. Apart from anything else, he's got my car keys and will not return them unless I say something complimentary.

(*Best Man*) and I have come through a lot of scraps. He's always been around for me, always ready to lend advice or give me a clip over the ear when I've needed it. I couldn't ask for a better friend, nor a more appropriate Best Man.

My last duty - and it's more a pleasure, I can assure you - is to thank the Bridesmaids. Anyone who can put up with the dramas and traumas of assisting in the organisation of a wedding deserves a medal! You look beautiful and I am indebted for the help you have given both to (*Bride*) and myself.

And so I would ask you all to be upstanding and raise your glasses...to the Bridesmaids.

SPEECH 6

Ladies and gentlemen, I would be lying if I didn't say I was nervous tonight - although not as nervous as I was this afternoon. After all, it's not every day you have such a vision of loveliness gliding down the aisle towards you - and that was only (*Bride's*) mother!

I'm still pinching myself when I look at (*Bride*) sitting here beside me. I feel like I've won Lotto. There's so much I want to say to you - but I can make it easy by simply saying I love you.

I must say I feel a little guilty taking (*Bride*) away from her mother and father.

I know they share a great

love for each other. I am privileged and honoured to now be a part of this close-knit circle.

From the very beginning I've been made to feel a part of (*Bride's*) family and it's a role I've enjoyed immensely.

On behalf of my parents, I would formally welcome (*Bride*) into our family.

I'm a great believer in family. I draw a lot of strength from mine, and now from (*Bride's*).

After today, I think I have an even greater appreciation of how important it is to have a loving family.

Everyone's pitched in unselfishly to make this day happen.

To both our mums and dads, and our extended families, thanks for everything you've done. It's been a very special day; one we'll never forget.

There are so many people to thank - stretching back from those who helped in the church today to the many friends who have offered advice and practical assistance over the last few months.

Forgive me if I thank you collectively - my gratitude is sincere, nonetheless.

A few people I must mention by name. (*Best Man*) and (*Groomsman*) have done a sterling job to get me here today. I can understand why a Groom needs a Best Man - it's impossible to pour yourself a stiff drink when you're shaking with nerves. Well, (*Best Man*) poured me that drink this morning - after which I poured him two of the same to settle him down. Seriously, though, I would like to thank the guys for being great mates and for making me the person that you see here tonight.

♦

Last, but by no means least, I want to thank our beautiful Bridesmaids. You could be forgiven for confusing these girls with Elle - in fact, I understand Elle wouldn't be here tonight because she didn't want to be outshone. Ladies, your beauty is matched only by your good grace. Both (*Bride*) and I thank you sincerely for all your help over the past months.

And so, without further ado, I would ask you to stand and join me in a toast to the Bridesmaids... to the Bridesmaids.

BRIDE

SPEECH 2

Ladies and gentlemen, Let me say from the outset that ours is a marriage of equals - and in that spirit, I am standing up to have my say.

(*Groom*) has already thanked both his parents and mine. I want to echo his sentiments - but please forgive me if I indulge momentarily with a special message to my Mum and Dad.

It's true to say that a bride's wedding day is just as special for her parents as it is for her. Mum has been fussing about me all day - as much to ensure I was ready as to hide her own jitters.

And as for dad - I'm not sure who was shaking more as we entered the church and started our walk down the aisle.

It's not often that I get an opportunity to thank them publicly for all they've done for me. I am the person you see before you today because of these two very special people.

They've instilled in me their values, given me an education and, most

64

♦

importantly, the confidence to tackle just about anything.

Mum and Dad, I love you both dearly and I thank you for everything, including this wonderful day.

I know it is (*Groom's*) duty to formally thank the bridesmaids - but they're my bridesmaids so I'm going to steal part of his thunder.

Girls, thanks for everything. I realised I'd chosen well on my hens night when you went out of your way to remove any temptation. I'm not going to say what you did with the temptations - that's our little secret.

Seriously, though, you've been a wonderful help in preparing for this day, and wonderful friends in every sense of the word.

Finally, I want to mention a very special person - (*Groom*).

It sounds silly to say I wouldn't be here without him - but it's true. (*Groom*), you've given me everything I could want - love, friendship, a future - and your bank book. You will live to regret the last.

I am looking forward to my life together with you and thank you for making me feel so special.

I do not want to overstay my welcome - so on that note, I thank you all once more and hand you back over to (*Groom*).

The Groom now finalises his speech and proposes the official toast to the bridesmaids.

BEST MAN

◆

As the Best Man, your role within the wedding party has been an important one.

Your speech is expected to be the least formal, thus giving you the maximum opportunity to express yourself.

There are a few things to keep in mind when writing your speech.

Think about how well you know the families of the bride and groom and the wedding guests.

This will establish how far you should go in your choice of jokes, anecdotes and humour.

No jokes, anecdotes or humour should be in bad taste.

Generally, all jokes should be at the expense of the groom, not the bride.

It is also your duty to reply on behalf of the bridesmaids.

You may then go on to thank the groom for selecting you as the best man.

It may also be up to you to read out any facsimiles or messages.

Sometimes the other groomsmen are involved in this and occasionally the ushers.

Ensure that you know the correct procedure before the wedding day.

Finally mention that your speech completes the formalities and indicate to the guests that you hope they will enjoy the rest of the evening!

SPEECH 1

Ladies and gentlemen,
George Bernard Shaw

once said: "Marriage is popular because it combines the maximum of temptation with the maximum of opportunity". **I** think he was absolutely right. I'm not short of temptation, especially tonight, seated at a table with so many beautiful ladies. But alas, NO OPPORTUNITY.

Trust (*Groom*) to get it right. (*Bride*) is definitely a temptation. I know, I have spent the past (?) months/years pursuing her. **B**ut just as I came close to success, (*Groom*) was always there ahead of me. **T**hen he has the audacity to ask me to be the "Best Man".

(*Bride*) I will now tell you a few home truths about your new husband.

(This is the time to include a few humorous anecdotes about the groom.)

Now (*Bride*), I hope you spend the rest of your life

◆

wishing you had married me. But if you had to miss out on the "Best Man" you couldn't have chosen better than (*Groom*).

He really has been a great mate and I am looking forward to being the third party on many of your romantic Saturday nights. **I** was told that it is my duty to reply on behalf of the bridesmaids and I know that if I get this wrong I will have them to answer to.

Thank you (*Groom*) for your kind words, these beautiful and elegant ladies certainly deserve your compliments. It has been a pleasure and an honour to look after them tonight.

There are several cards and messages, addressed to the bride and groom, so I would like to call upon the groomsmen to join me here to share them with you.

(Read out any messages and telegrams, avoiding any that are in bad taste.)
I started with the wise words of a great man, and I intend to finish the same way. These words express the way I feel about marriage, and to let *(Groom)* know that I think he has chosen wisely. In the words of Samuel Johnson "Marriage has many pains, but celibacy has no pleasures".
(Pretend to cry a few tears, then recover just as quickly.)
The formalities are now over and I hope you enjoy the rest of the evening. Ladies and gentlemen, thank you.

SPEECH 2

Note: This is a short succinct speech for the Best Man who doesn't have the confidence for a long speech, or doesn't know many people at the wedding. This speech is purposefully serious and formal.

Ladies and gentlemen,
It was my great honour to be asked by *(Groom)* to be his Best Man, today.
I have known *(Groom)* for many years in which time we have become really great mates.
(Groom) has always conducted his life with the highest values of morality and integrity. This is evident by the many wonderful friends that have gathered here today. They say you can judge a man by the company he keeps. Well if there is any truth in this then *(Groom)* may be well judged.
(Bride) is a fantastic person and I feel that they are terribly well suited.
I have really enjoyed meeting all of *(Bride and Groom's)* family and

friends, mostly for the first time. I am honoured to meet so many wonderful people and I look forward to speaking to everyone tonight.

It is my very pleasant duty to thank (*Groom*) for his kind words, so appropriately expressed to the bridesmaids. They really do look magnificent.

There seem to be quite a few letters and notes expressing the best of good wishes to the bride and groom, so I would like to share these with you now....

(*Read out any telegrams and messages - avoiding any in bad taste.*)

Well, ladies and gentlemen, the night's formalities have now ended, I hope you enjoy the rest of the evening, and I expect to see you all on the dance floor shortly.

...Thank you.

SPEECH 3

Ladies and gentlemen, Firstly, I must begin with an apology; I'm sorry if I embarrassed anyone during the photo session.

How was I to know what the photographer meant when he said "A quick flash of the Best Man" (*Cover your eyes briefly in a mock gesture.*)

After that experience, all the guests should know who I am, in great detail, I'm sure.

Yes, I'm the Best Man. The "Best" that is. I've never really understood the title. If I'm supposed to be the Best Man than how come (*Groom*) gets the girl.

While we're on the subject, let's talk about (*Groom*). (*Groom*) and I have been close mates for many years.

When (*Groom*) asked me to be his Best Man at this

♦

wedding I was really excited. Then he told me about this speech. Oh no! The nerves crept in. My stomach fell to the floor and in fact arrived at the reception about half an hour after I did. I have been quivering and quaking at the knees for weeks. (*Groom*) has been exactly the same.

We have racked our brains as to what to say. We have spent many, and I mean, many nervous nights talking about what we should say. Then suddenly this morning it dawned on me. I have only one question for you, Ladies and Gentlemen:

How come (*Groom*) is more nervous about his wedding speech than his wedding night? (*Pause*) I suppose we'll have to let the newly-weds answer that one.

I have really enjoyed myself today. This has been a wonderful occasion.

I wish to thank (*Bride and Groom's*) parents for the obvious time and effort to make us all feel so welcome.

(*Bride's Parents*) should always remember, that they haven't lost a daughter, just gained another problem.

It is also my honoured duty to reply on behalf of the bridesmaids. In fact they are store mannequins and can't really talk. This is why I have been asked to speak for them. I'll spend the rest of the night answering to that one.

(*Groom's*) words about the bridesmaids couldn't be more aptly expressed.

They really do look magnificent and too good to be real.

As to the newly-weds, I have never met a couple more committed to each other and their future lives

together. They have it all worked out. From the day they first looked into each others eyes, until today, theirs has truly been a match made in heaven. Finally, Janos Arany so cloquently said: "In dreams and in love there are no impossibilities" I'm sure with the determination, compatibility and love that (*Bride and Groom*) have for each other, there will be no impossibilities in their future life together. I'd like to take some time now to read the notes and good wishes that have been sent by people unable to attend this wonderful occasion.
(*Read notes and telegrams, avoiding any that are unsuitable.*)
Well, ladies and gentlemen, it is now time to relax, let your hair down and enjoy the rest of the evening....Thank you.

SPEECH 4

Ladies and gentlemen, It's very appropriate that (*Groom*) is getting married somewhat later in life. After all, he's never been on time for anything. If it wasn't for me, we'd probably still be waiting in the church for him now. It's not that he's slow off the mark. Once he sets his mind on something, that's it. After all, he snapped (*Bride*) up pretty quickly - and that's no mean feat. Looking at her tonight, you can just imagine the competition he must have faced. As for me, I was never in the race - you might say I retired hurt (*look wistfully towards the bride*).
So why is he always late? It's not that he's lazy - although you just wait, (*Bride*), till you try to get him working around the house.

♦

Take it from me - he thinks a nail is something that lives on the end of your finger. And the only screwdriver he's ever been known to handle is in a long, tall glass.

It's not that he's particularly stupid - although he did choose me as his Best Man, knowing full well that I would spend five minutes dumping on him.

No, I'd have to say that (*Groom*) has a pretty relaxed nature. He gets to where he's going in his own good time. And I guess that's one of the real strengths of his character - unflappable, steadfast and good-natured.

He's a good man to have around in a crisis. I mean, who else could have let down the hem on my wedding trousers ten minutes before zero hour. In all seriousness, I want to say that I am honoured to have been chosen as (*Groom's*) Best Man. We've been friends for a great many years - more than I care to remember. Friends like (*Groom*) do not come along every day. I am proud to know him, and prouder of the choice he has made today.

After all, marriage is a wonderful institution - didn't Zza Zza Gabor say that?

Congratulations (*Bride*). You deserve every happiness and I know that (*Groom*) will deliver to you that happiness.

On behalf of the ladies sitting across the table from me, I would like to thank (*Groom*) for his toast. I do, however, take umbrage with what he said - our bridesmaids are far more beautiful than you expressed, you cad!

Ladies and gentlemen, I have nothing more to say but congratulations to

(Bride and Groom).
Thank you for your kind attention and please enjoy the remainder of the evening.

SPEECH 5

Ladies and gentlemen, I've spent the last couple of weeks thinking a lot about this speech. I've tried to think of jokes and anecdotes that belittle *(Groom)*.

After all, that's what a Best Man's speech is supposed to do, isn't it?

But in the end, I've decided to follow a more serious course. You see, in my deliberations I've been thinking a lot about the nature of friendship.

It seems to me that friendship is all about trust - about being there for someone at any time, in any circumstances, and knowing you can rely on that person in return.

It's about respect - instinctively knowing how far you can go without stepping on toes.

And it's about honesty and acceptance - putting aside the little surface faults and judging the real person below.

My relationship with *(Groom)* is built on these platforms.

He has been a friend to me in every sense of the word and it has been an honour and a pleasure to call him my friend.

At this moment I am very proud of *(Groom)*.

He deserves all the happiness and blessings that have been bestowed on him this day.

I congratulate his bride, *(Bride)*.

Because I know *(Groom)* so well, I know you have a man who will show you the trust, respect, honesty and acceptance that he has shown me over the years.

And I feel I know you well enough to say that it will be returned in kind. Thank you both for allowing me the honour of sharing your special day.

I also have the honour of speaking on behalf of our bridesmaids in thanking *(Groom)* for his kind words when proposing their toast.

I do not really need to add anything to what *(Groom)* said about how beautiful the girls look. In fact, they look so good that *(Groomsman)* and I sort of pale beside them. *(With mock indignation)* Thanks very much, girls! Nevertheless, I know they would want me to thank you both for doing them the honour of including them in your bridal party. Ladies and gentlemen, I've said enough. Thank you for your kind attention throughout the speeches and please continue to enjoy the hospitality of our hosts...Thank you.

SPEECH 6

Ladies and gentlemen, To say I'm nervous is an understatement. I would have had a stiff drink before I got up - but I couldn't hold the glass. I'm not as nervous as *(Groom)* was a few minutes ago, though. He couldn't even SEE his glass.

This afternoon, on our way to the church, he was particularly nervous. *(Groom)*, who was driving, had the car kangaroo-hopping into the church yard. Not a bad effort, when you consider the car's an automatic. *(Bride)*, you were probably wondering why he was standing so stiffly at the head of the aisle when you arrived. We had a broom handle stuck up the back of his coat to keep him from falling over.

He was just as nervous last week on his buck's night. I can't imagine why.

The reality is, his mates were too scared to do anything to him, for fear of what his fiancée would do to them if they touched a hair on his head.

(Bride), I'd just like to say right here and now that we had nothing to do with the hangover he was sporting the following day. It was totally self-inflicted.

Putting aside his nervous nature for just one moment, I would like to say that it's been an honour to stand with *(Groom)* today on what is the most important day of his life.

I am very proud to call him a friend, and even more proud of what he's done with his life.

I think everyone here would agree that *(Groom and Bride)* are a perfect match. First and foremost, they are friends - and as far as I can see, that is the most important foundation of a good marriage.

I can only see a happy and prosperous life ahead for you both - and that's no more than you deserve.

On behalf of the bridesmaids, I would like to thank *(Groom)* for his kind words. They would like me to convey, I'm sure, their gratitude and appreciation for being a part of your special day.

Well, I'm just about over my stage fright - so much so, that I feel I could stand up here and talk for another ten minutes.

Would anyone like to hear about the joys of stamp collecting? No?

Well in that case, I will thank you for your kind attention and invite you to enjoy the rest of the evening...

THE WEDDING

◆

The following pages provide you with everything you could possibly need to practise, write and execute the wedding speech that you have been asked, or are required, to deliver!

By using the checklists provided and recording every relevant detail, you will assure that no one has been overlooked.

Especially the many people that require special thanks!

We trust that this book has made the job of giving your speech a little easier and helps you to "rise to the occasion" with confidence on the day.

We wish you every success!

WEDDING DATE:

_____

CEREMONY VENUE:

_____

RECEPTION VENUE:

_____

PHONE NUMBER:

_____

ADDRESS:

_____

_____

_____

OFFICIATOR:

_____

PHONE NUMBER:

_____

ADDRESS:

_____

_____

_____

_____

BRIDE:

_____

HOME PHONE:

_____

WORK PHONE:

_____

ADDRESS:

_____

_____

_____

_____

BRIDE'S MOTHER:

_____

HOME PHONE:

_____

WORK PHONE:

_____

GROOM'S FATHER:

_____

HOME PHONE:

_____

WORK PHONE:

_____

ADDRESS:

_____

_____

_____

_____

GROOM:

_____

HOME PHONE:

_____

WORK PHONE:

_____

ADDRESS:

_____

_____

_____

_____

GROOM'S MOTHER:

_____

HOME PHONE:

_____

WORK PHONE:

_____

GROOM'S FATHER:

_____

HOME PHONE:

_____

WORK PHONE:

_____

ADDRESS:

_____

_____

_____

_____

CHIEF BRIDESMAID:	BEST MAN:
_____	_____
PHONE NUMBER:	PHONE NUMBER:
_____	_____
BRIDESMAID:	GROOMSMAN:
_____	_____
PHONE NUMBER:	PHONE NUMBER:
_____	_____
BRIDESMAID:	GROOMSMAN:
_____	_____
PHONE NUMBER:	PHONE NUMBER:
_____	_____
BRIDESMAID:	GROOMSMAN:
_____	_____
PHONE NUMBER:	PHONE NUMBER:
_____	_____
FLOWER GIRL:	PAGE BOY:
_____	_____
PHONE NUMBER:	PHONE NUMBER:
_____	_____

~ If you are in any doubt as to the correct pronunciation of the names of the people in your speech, simply get on the telephone, ring that person and ask. It is better to do this before the wedding than to sound foolish on the day. People will appreciate your interest and your speech will sound personal and sincere. ~

ORDER OF TOASTS & SPEECHES

♦

Here we allow you to note the order of speakers for the reception you are to attend.

In conference with the bride and groom you should detail carefully who and when each speaker will appear.

We have also included the traditional order of toasts and speeches for your reference, but remember this sequence is not always followed so ensure that you include any changes. These may include the mother of the bride, the bride, or any other person of choice.

Knowing the order of the speeches before the day will ensure that all proceeds smoothly.

MASTER OF CEREMONY:
The M.C. controls the overall flow of events and begins by politely calling the guests to attention. The Best Man is sometimes asked to act as the M.C.

FIRST SPEAKER:
Traditionally the Father of the Bride delivers the first speech.

FIRST TOAST:
Traditionally the Father of the Bride offers the first toast of the day to the bride and groom.

SECOND SPEAKER:
Traditionally the Groom is the second speaker of the day, responding to the Father of the Bride.

SECOND TOAST:
Traditionally the Groom proposes the second toast

at the end of his speech.
He proposes a toast to the bridesmaids, thanking them for their support extended to the Bride.

THIRD SPEAKER:

Traditionally the Best Man speaks after the Groom. It is his duty to reply on behalf of the bridesmaids. He thanks the groom for asking him to be best man and gives a speech.

THIRD TOAST:

At the conclusion of his speech, the Best Man may return the proceedings to the M.C. or if he is to perform this duty, offers a toast to the bride's parents.

FOURTH TOAST:

The Father of the Bride will respond to the third toast, thanking the Best Man or M.C and all present. He will then propose a toast to the Groom's parents. He will then return the proceedings to the M.C. or Best Man who will read

out any messages received from people unable to attend the reception. After this is concluded the M.C. will finalise the proceedings by inviting the guests to enjoy the rest of the evening.

MASTER OF CEREMONIES:

_____

FIRST SPEAKER:

_____

SECOND SPEAKER:

_____

THIRD SPEAKER:

_____

FOURTH SPEAKER:

_____

FIFTH SPEAKER:

_____

SIXTH SPEAKER:

_____

SEVENTH SPEAKER:

_____

EIGHTH SPEAKER:

_____

IMPORTANT INFORMATION

Use this page to detail any important information that the bride, groom or their families would like you to include in your speech.

For example:

♦ Names to remember.
♦ Introductions.
♦ Special Thank you's.
♦ Messages
♦ Stories

_____

_____

_____

_____

_____

_____

_____

_____

_____

_____

_____

_____

_____

_____

_____

_____

_____

_____

_____

_____

_____

_____

_____

_____

_____

_____

_____

_____

_____

_____

MY SPEECH

◆

OPENING LINE

_____

_____

_____

_____

_____

CONTENT

_____

_____

_____

_____

_____

_____

_____

_____

_____

_____

_____

_____

_____

_____

_____

CONTENT

_____

_____

_____

_____

_____

_____

_____

_____

_____

_____

_____

_____

_____

_____

_____

_____

_____

_____

_____

_____

_____

_____

_____

_____

_____

_____

_____

_____

_____

_____

CONTENT

CLOSING LINE

_____
_____
_____
_____
_____
_____
_____
_____
_____
_____
_____
_____

TOAST

_____
_____
_____
_____
_____
_____
_____
_____
_____
_____
_____
_____

NOTES

Also produced by the publishers:

The BRIDE'S DIARY

Australia's Leading Bridal Publication

Australia's leading bridal publication: *The Bride's Diary* is your complete planner and guide to wedding etiquette. This is a unique hard-covered publication of the highest quality and elegance, featuring gold throughout.

The Bride's Diary is designed to be your ultimate assistant. From the time of your engagement through to buying your first home, this is a complete guide to traditional wedding etiquette as well as offering many contemporary ideas.

For your convenience the rear section of the book is a workable diary, including comprehensive checklists, budget planners and even a calendar enabling you to record ideas, services you have engaged and important details like your "guest and gift list" as well as your "thank you" list.

The highly reputable and professional companies represented in *The Bride's Diary* are all experts in their chosen field. We are confident that they are as anxious as we are to ensure your special day is completely perfect.

By using *The Bride's Diary* as your planner you can be totally relaxed and confident about your wedding day and you will also have a distinctive and elegant memento to keep as a reminder of one of life's truly great occasions.

To order your copy of The Bride's Diary simply fill out your state coupon below, include a personal cheque, bank cheque or postal money order for the amount specified and post to the address shown on the coupon.

Name_____

Address_____

_____State____Post Code____

State Edition Required: ❐ **Victoria** ❐**Victoria Country**
Post this coupon with payment for **$ 9.95** (includes p&p) to:
Worsthorne Publishing. PO Box 261 Mt Eliza Victoria 3930

Name_____

Address_____

_____State____Post Code____

State Edition Required: ❐ **N.S.W.** ❐ **Qld.** ❐ **S.A.** ❐ **A.C.T.**
Post this coupon with payment for **$ 12.50** (larger A4 format)
(includes p&p) to: **Worsthorne Pedersen Publishing Pty Ltd.**
PO Box 834 Bowral NSW 2576